WHERE I AM LED
A Service Exploration Workbook

Christina Parker

Where I Am Led

A Service Exploration Workbook

Christina Parker

Alfred Press
Hubbardston, Massachusetts

Alfred Press
12 Simond Hill Road
Hubbardston, MA 01452

Where I Am Led:
A Service Exploration Workbook
©2009 Christina Parker

ISBN 978-0-578-03595-6

All rights reserved.
No part of this book may be reproduced in any form
or by any means without the permission of the author.

Printed in cooperation with
Lulu Enterprises, Inc.
860 Aviation Parkway, Suite 300
Morrisville, NC 27560

This book is dedicated to my parents who always encouraged me to be whatever I wanted to be, to Master Scott who provided the first beacon of light in the darkness of my path and gave me the strength and inspiration to follow that light, to Master Todd who gave me the tools and strength to see the colors and explore the shadows as I travel, and to Fletcher who taught me how to accept the help of others along the way.

***

I would like to gratefully acknowledge the assistance of Raven Kaldera and Joshua Tenpenny in producing this book.

Table of Contents

Preface: Honoring the Past 1
Introduction 3
How to Use this Book 4
Writing Assignment #1: Role Models 9
Monthly Practical Project #1: Nutrition and Meal Planning 10
Writing Assignment #2: Most Valuable Asset 13
Writing Assignment #3: Overcoming a Limit 16
Writing Assignment #4: Indirect Service 19
Writing Assignment #5: Emotional Fulfillment 22
Monthly Practical Project #2: Leather Care 23
Writing Assignment #6: Entertainment 26
Writing Assignment #7: Characteristics Essential for Ownership 29
Writing Assignment #8: Personal Fantasy 32
Writing Assignment #9: Self-Improvement 35
Monthly Practical Project #3: Travel Planning 36
Writing Assignment #10: Reality Check 39
Writing Assignment #11: A Song in Your Heart 42
Writing Assignment #12: The Infamous Car Analogy Question 45
Writing Assignment #13: More Fantasy Exploration 48
Monthly Practical Project #4: Compiling a Packing List 49
Writing Assignment #14: The Joy of Service 52
Writing Assignment #15: In-depth Exploration—Integrity 55
Writing Assignment #16: First Impressions 58
Writing Assignment #17: Receiving Compliments 61
Writing Assignment #18: Memory Lane 64
Monthly Practical Project #5: Horticulture 65
Writing Assignment #19: Real Role Models 68
Writing Assignment #20: In-depth Exploration—Vulnerability 71
Writing Assignment #21: In-Depth Exploration—Honor 74
Writing Assignment #22: Happiness 77
Monthly Practical Project #6: Budgeting and Economizing 78
Writing Assignment #23: A Song in My Heart—Part Two 81
Writing Assignment #24: Self-Image 84
Writing Assignment #25: First Impressions—Part Two 87
Writing Assignment #26: Gratitude List 90
Monthly Practical Project #7: Party Planning 91
Writing Assignment #27: Accomplishments 94
Writing Assignment #28: In-depth Exploration—Usefulness 97
Writing Assignment #29: Once Upon a Time… 100
Writing Assignment #30: Teachers 103

Writing Assignment #31: Self-Knowledge 106
Monthly Practical Project #8: Dungeon Decor 107
Writing Assignment #32: Dream Job 110
Writing Assignment #33: Book Report 113
Writing Assignment #34: Physical Delights 116
Writing Assignment #35: Fantasy Owner 119
Monthly Practical Project #9: Preparing to Attend a Leather Event 120
Writing Assignment #36: A Different Perspective 123
Writing Assignment #37: In-depth Exploration—Respect 126
Writing Assignment #38: Physical Examination 129
Writing Assignment #39: Say What? 132
Monthly Practical Project #10: Fetish Attire 133
Writing Assignment #40: Seven Little Words 136
Writing Assignment #41: Civil Disobedience? 139
Writing Assignment #42: Submission and Surrender 142
Writing Assignment #43: Love 145
Monthly Practical Project #11: Single-tail Whips 146
Writing Assignment #44: You've Got Personality! 149
Writing Assignment #45: The Gift of Giving 152
Writing Assignment #46: Taking a Stand 155
Writing Assignment #47: Peace 158
Writing Assignment #48: Santa's Workshop 161
Monthly Practical Project #12: Basic Massage Skills 162
Writing Assignment #49: In-depth Exploration—Obedience 165
Writing Assignment #50: Print or Film? 168
Writing Assignment #51: Rebellion 171
Writing Assignment #52: Looking Back 175
Choosing To Serve 176

Preface:
Honoring the Past

(This is the introduction to the earlier form of this workbook, The Path of Service—Guideposts for Excellence. *I have included it here as it was originally published in its entirety. My life and relationships have changed dramatically since this piece was written but this remains part of the foundation I stand upon today. I have no wish to deny or edit my past since I am as proud of where I've been as I am of where am I going.)*

Five years ago, Master Todd gave me the assignment to write one thought about service or submission a day for five weeks. (OK, it was part of a punishment, but do we really need to go into that part?) After one week of writing the thoughts, I asked permission to have the assignment extended indefinitely since it was proving to be extremely beneficial to me. I continued writing the thoughts for a few more months, and then life got in the way and I put them aside. I had always intended to pick them back up again when I had the time, but I never managed to find that time.

A little over four years later, I was presenting my workshop entitled "Becoming a Prized Possession". After the workshop, several people in the audience asked if I would send them the notes for my presentation. Since the only written materials for my workshops are broad outlines that only I would understand, I thought I would be unable to fulfill their request, but then I remembered the thoughts I had written so many years ago. So I told them that I might have something useful for them and promised to send what I could.

When I went to pull out my old "thoughts", I expected to be a little embarrassed by a look at my naiveté after so many years of growth and exploration as a slave. To my surprise, I found that in spite of the years of experience and understanding I had gained, they were just as valid for me today as they were when I wrote them five years ago. However, even though the years had not changed my opinions, I realized there were many things that I could add to what I had originally written.

I had often been asked the question, "When are you going to write a book?" Looking at the thoughts from five years previous and feeling the inspiration to add to those thoughts, I faced the inevitable conclusion that the answer to that question was "Now".

Slavery is a lifestyle choice but it is also a journey and I have been blessed with the opportunity to learn from some of the best tour guides the leather community has to offer. While the thoughts in this book are my own, I had many sources of inspiration for them. First of all, I would like to thank the women I consider to be my first tour guides—Molly Devon, Vi Johnson, Laura Antoniou, and Karen Taylor. They came into my life at a pivotal point in my journey and their recognition and matter of fact acceptance of my slavery enabled me to accept it within myself. Of course, the journey would be very lonely without my traveling companions—ronda, dave, kimmie, debbie, gypsie, sheryl, pug, chris Z., Patrick, lacey, nadine, sugar, tony, and all of the other slaves, submissives, girls and boys who have shared their joys, sorrows, questions and insights with me over the years. In addition to tour guides and traveling companions, I have been blessed with a wonderful family of choice who give me the strength and courage to keep moving forward when the path gets hard to follow—Ms. Kristine, robert, Master Steve Sampson and family, Master Skip Chasey and family, and others mentioned above. However, out of all the blessings and inspiration I have received on my journey, the two greatest are the men I am privileged to serve—Master Scott and Master Todd.

Since I view slavery and service as a journey, I have written this book to serve as guideposts to help mark out a path for that journey over the course of a year. The path for each person will be different and yours will not always match the one laid out in this book. I have tried to make this book useful to all service-oriented people, whether you are currently in service or preparing yourself for the day when you will surrender to the one you will serve. Although it was specifically written for slaves, it is my hope that anyone who chooses the path of service will find something of value within these pages. Completion of this book over the course of a year does not constitute a beginning or an end to the journey; it simply indicates an exploration of a portion of the path. Above all, my goal for this book is to assist slaves in developing the most valuable assets they have to offer in service—their mind, heart and soul.

Even though I identify as a heterosexual female slave, I have tried to make this book as inclusive as possible of all slaves regardless of gender or orientation. I debated long and hard about the terms and labels I would use in this book. Although I view the term "Master" as gender-neutral, I recognize that this usage has not been universally embraced by the leather community. Also, I know slaves who serve people who identify as Sirs, Ma'ams, Mommies, and Daddies as well as those who identify as Master or Mistress. The common factor to all of these identities is the concept of ownership. Therefore, I finally settled on the term "Owner" to refer to the person the slave has committed to serving. It may not be as sexy, but it is certainly better than a string of labels separated by slashes.

Introduction

When I published the first version of this workbook, I had no idea how people would react to it. This is definitely a book designed to be "written by the reader"—a workbook with an emphasis on the "work" part of that word. My goal then (and now) was to create a tool for self-exploration. I knew that there was a certain amount of value in the "book" part because just reading it offers a glimpse of what it means to serve, but I wasn't sure if anyone would find value in the "work" part. I was thrilled that the response to the book has been so positive. However, I began to feel a heightened sense of responsibility when it became clear that people were actually doing the work outlined in the book. These people were making a huge commitment of time and energy and I wanted to make sure that they had the best tool I could provide to help them complete it.

With that thought in mind, I began thinking of ways to expand and refine the content. Initially, I thought there may be one or two parts of the book that people would find little or no value in completing. From the feedback I received, it quickly became clear that everyone had particular preferences but parts that some people didn't like, others loved. I had a few people suggest various ways to organize the material, but the majority liked the fairly random placement of the exercises. I'll admit, I was gratified by the majority opinion since it supports my belief that life circumstances change and our needs do not follow a carefully planned and structured progression—sometimes we need to go back to the basics and sometimes we find ourselves in a marathon when we're still learning to walk.

Many things have changed in my life since I wrote the first edition of this workbook, and it was only after I finished the revisions that I realized how closely the changes in my life and this book mirror each other. On the outside, my life looks completely different than it did three years ago—and, like this book, most people knew me by another name. Once you get past the outer layers, however, the changes become less noticeable. There are some additions (the guideposts and an article) but with the exception of a few "tweaks" here and there, the core content remains the same. On the other hand, if the book appears more organized, that is due to the work done by Raven and Joshua of Alfred Press and not a sign of any growth from me in that area.

If there is anything else that needs to be included in this introduction, I think the following story covers it. Out of all the comments and dialogues I've had regarding this workbook, there is one that stands out among all of the others as a clear indication that I had accomplished exactly what I set out to do when I created it. Everything happened so quickly that the details are a little fuzzy, but here is what I remember.

I was waiting for an elevator during a Master/slave-focused event and had a copy of the book in my hands. A woman went rushing by, then stopped suddenly and turned around to look at me. She asked me if I had written the book and when I said that I had, she replied, "I hate you, but I love you. I hate the book, but I love it—thanks." Then she turned back around and left to complete whatever urgent mission she'd interrupted to share her thoughts with me. I still smile when I think about it. Trust a slave to put the "work" in workbook—and trust another slave to appreciate the effort.

How to Use this Book

There are four distinct parts to this book—monthly practical projects, weekly guideposts, twice-weekly "thoughts", and weekly writing assignments. At the end of the book is a bonus article entitled *Choosing to Serve*. The purpose of each part is to provide tools for self-exploration and skill development.

Monthly Practical Projects

These projects are designed to help you develop skills that will increase your usefulness to your Owner. While you may never put into practical application the specific projects you complete, you will have many opportunities to apply the skills you will develop as you complete the projects. For example, you might not ever be called into service as a landscape designer, but you will probably be called upon to utilize the research and budgeting skills you develop while performing assignments 5 and 6.

I have not included space in this book for you to write all of your project reports in it, but I strongly encourage you to write out all of your work when you do the practical projects. You might want to get a three-ring binder to keep all of the information and results from the monthly projects in one place. The act of putting into words what you have learned or plotting out on paper the specifics of the plan you have developed will help solidify the knowledge you have gained. It will also give you additional opportunities to develop your writing and planning skills. Use the space provided to write notes on the resources you used and the points you want to be sure to remember later. (Examples: "Miss Longnose's Party Planning Guide—useful checklists and recipe ideas" or "Make sure to pack Owner's allergy medication for springtime vacations.")

Weekly Guideposts

These are single words associated with the concepts of service. For each word, I've provided a short quote (either my own words or those from famous dead people no longer subject to copyright laws). These quotes are meant to be a starting point for exploration of the concept. What images or emotions come to mind when you think about the guidepost word? Do you have any examples from your own life that help define the concept for you? Keep the guidepost word in mind as you go through your week and use the space provided to make notes, write out your experiences, or create your own quotes inspired by the guidepost word.

Twice-Weekly "Thoughts"

The "thoughts" in this book are bits of advice and insight I have gathered on my own journey. I encourage you to use the space provided in this book to write a comment about each one. Do you agree with what I have written? Do you disagree with it? Does what I have written remind you of a specific incident you've experienced? Do you have additional comments to add to what I have written? The type of response you make is not important. What is important is that you think about what I have written and compose your own unique response.

Weekly Writing Assignments

The weekly writing assignments are designed to assist you in self-exploration while focusing that exploration in positive directions. I encourage you to be as detailed as possible when you are completing the assignments. The act of searching out the additional details will lead you into areas you had not previously thought to explore within yourself.

These assignments are also designed to assist your Owner in understanding who you are and what you want to be. If you are currently in service, I encourage you to share your work in all parts of this book with your Owner but most especially your completed writing assignments. If you are not currently in service, I encourage you to view the writing assignments as a way to explain yourself to the Owner you will eventually wish to serve.

General Advice

In between the monthly practical projects, the weekly writing assignments, the twice weekly thoughts, and the guideposts are an awful lot of blank lines. Your journey exists on those lines. They are the keys to finding your way on the path from one signpost to the next. You can skip between the signposts without writing a single thought or completing a single assignment, but you will only be sightseeing on my path and not forging your own.

It might be helpful if you work on this book with a group. Whether it is with an established club or just a couple of friends, sharing the experience with others may keep you moving forward when you might otherwise stop. Remember, misery shared is halved, while joy shared is doubled.

Important Reminder

The gender-neutral terms "Owner" and "slave" used in this book are intended to be inclusive of *anyone* who receives or gives service respectively. Please substitute the label of your choice for these roles as you use this book.

A Note To Owners

This book could be the most valuable resource you will ever have in guiding the person who serves you. The writing assignments and comments on the weekly thoughts will give you insight into what feeds and motivates your slave. I strongly encourage you to routinely read and discuss with your slave what he or she has written within these pages. Your ongoing interest will remind your slave that this self-exploration is a service to you, and provide incentive for your slave to keep working through the book even when it is inconvenient or difficult to do.

A Final Note for slaves

While it isn't clear in most of this book, I have a highly (sometimes overly) developed sense of humor. Yes, the journey is hard at times and requires a great deal of work, but it is not worth taking that first step if you are not going to have fun along the way. So, if in the course of completing this book you start to feel like it is too hard or too much work, feel free to let your own sense of humor take over and have a little fun with the assignments. Be irreverent. Be sarcastic. I won't be reading your comments—and there is a good chance I would agree with them if I did.

Happy Trails!

> ## Guidepost #1
> ## Determination
> Determination can often turn a failure into a success. There are many ways to accomplish the same goal. If one way doesn't work, try another until you find one that does.

Comments:

Thoughts for the Week:

> Many people make the mistake of assuming that giving up control also means giving up responsibility. No matter what the situation, a slave shares equal responsibility for any consequences, either good or bad, that occur as a result of consensual activities.

Comments:

> There is a strong power that can be gained through surrender. It is not a power that comes from manipulation or passive-aggressive control over another person. Instead, it is a peaceful, internal power that fills the heart and soul of the slave who recognizes the pleasure that quiet obedience gives to an owner.

Comments:

Writing Assignment #1
Role Models

Name three fictional characters who would be good role models for an aspiring slave and explain why.

Monthly Practical Project #1
Nutrition and Meal Planning

Your Owner has decided to add "dietician" to your list of responsibilities. Your assignment for this project is to prepare a meal plan for a one-week period. This meal plan should accommodate your Owner's preferences, dietary restrictions and budget considerations. Consider how often your Owner likes to eat and the amount of food your Owner normally consumes at each meal. Your goal should be to create a meal plan that provides variety and nutrition while appealing to your Owner's taste buds. If you are not currently in service, imagine that your Owner was just advised to start a heart-healthy diet.

Research tool suggestions:
- Cookbooks
- Nutrition Websites
- Meal planning websites

Ideas and Resources:

> **Guidepost #2**
> **Obedience**
> Obedience means much more than just following orders. To be truly obedient, you must be just as committed to following orders that are a burden to you as you are to those that are a joy.

Comments:

Thoughts for the Week:

> Never assume that something is allowed just because it is not expressly forbidden. For example, an order to be respectful to all Owners does not imply permission to be disrespectful to all others.

Comments:

> It is often said that slaves should never be proud. This does not mean that slaves should not gain self-esteem and satisfaction from the progress they have made and their accomplishments. The danger of self-pride in a slave is complacency. By remaining humble, a slave will continue to strive for further growth.

Comments:

Writing Assignment #2
Most Valuable Asset

What do you feel is the most valuable asset you have to offer your Owner? Explain why.

> **Guidepost #3**
> **Patience**
> Exceptional service requires exceptional patience. Have faith, focus on what is happening in the present, and the rest will follow.

Comments:

Thoughts for the Week:

> Consent is not something to be given lightly. By giving consent to any activity – whether done by the slave or to the slave – the slave is making a pledge to the Owner. This pledge of consent allows the Owner to expect the slave to accept the consequences of the activity. It also implies consent to punishment for any failure to live up to that pledge.

Comments:

> Striving to be a "low maintenance" slave is an admirable goal, and one way to achieve this goal is to minimize the number of complaints you make to your Owner. Keep in mind, however, that some concerns are legitimate and need to be addressed as soon as possible. A good rule of thumb to follow is to ask yourself, "Will this bother me tomorrow?" If the answer is no, then you should let it drop. If the answer is yes, then you have an obligation to discuss the situation with your Owner rather than harbor a resentment that will create a barrier to the trust you have built together.

Comments:

Writing Assignment #3
Overcoming a Limit

Name one limit that you have consensually overcome. Why was it a limit and what enabled you to overcome it?

> **Guidepost #4**
> **Courtesy**
> Just as doors work better when oil is applied to the hinges, people work better when courtesy is extended to them. A moment spent being courteous now can save you hours of time repairing the damage later.

Comments:

Thoughts for the Week:

> Loyalty to your Owner requires much more than merely submitting only to your Owner (or others that your Owner has specified). Loyalty requires that you give your Owner the benefit of the doubt when questions arise. Loyalty also requires that a slave must share concerns or complaints with his or her Owner before sharing those problems with others.

Comments:

> While it is admirable and desirable for a slave to break down barriers and stretch limits as a demonstration of trust and submission, be careful not to go farther or faster than you are ready to go. Try to be as honest and realistic with yourself as you possibly can. Some limits will be permanent, but others can be eliminated as the trust you have in your Owner gives you the courage to tackle them and explore what lies on the other side. Let that trust help you overcome your fears and – when you are no longer afraid – you will find it easy and natural to move forward.

Comments:

Writing Assignment #4
Indirect Service

Indirect service is something that benefits or pleases your Owner that does not include interacting directly with your Owner, list ten ways that you can indirectly serve your Owner.

> **Guidepost #5**
> **Learning**
> It is the people who can do nothing who can find nothing to do, and the secret of happiness in this world is not only to be useful, but to be forever elevating one's usefulness.   -Sandra Orne Jewett

Comments:

Thoughts for the Week:

> When I think about the awesome responsibility that accepting control of another human being entails, I am humbled. To know that someone believes that this burden is worth shouldering in order to have my submission is a precious gift. It is that state of humility which urges me to continue to improve the quality of my service so that I might ease the burden of Ownership.

Comments:

> By surrender of my body, my spirit is set free.

Comments:

Writing Assignment #5
Emotional Fulfillment

Name three things that you need in order to be emotionally fulfilled by your service and explain why.

Monthly Practical Project #2
Leather Care

While some Owners like to perform their leather care tasks themselves, most Owners would rather have their slaves take on that responsibility. This month's assignment is to learn the basics of leather care for boots, toys and clothing. In addition to learning how to care for different items and different types of leather, you should put together a list of products and tools necessary to properly care for your Owner's leather.

If you are a bootblack or are already familiar with the basics of leather care, your assignment will be to acquire at least two new advanced leather care skills. These skills can be anything from repairing damaged leather (tears, spots, etc.) to making leather items that would be of interest to your Owner.

Research tool suggestions:
- Bootblack websites
- Boot manufacturer websites
- Leather care product websites
- Leather supplier websites
- Toy-maker websites

Ideas and Resources:

> **Guidepost #6**
> **Understanding**
> One of the greatest gifts you can give another person is the gift of understanding. To give this gift, you must look beneath the surface to the truth that lies within.

Comments:

Thoughts for the Week:

> A valuable talent for a slave to have is the ability to anticipate and fulfill an Owner's needs, wants, and desires. This "talent" is actually a learned skill that is acquired by remaining focused on your Owner and observant of even the slightest facial expression. Watching your Owner interact with others can be especially enlightening. What traits does your Owner find pleasing in others? What topics of conversation fascinate your Owner? Are these things you can incorporate into your service?

Comments:

> Remember, Ownership is as much a consensual activity as slavery. An Owner needs to earn trust and respect before gaining that priceless gift of surrender. A slave also needs to earn that same level of trust and respect before expecting to have that gift accepted.

Comments:

Writing Assignment #6
Entertainment

Entertainment is a form of service. Describe a time when you provided entertainment for the person you were serving.

> **Guidepost #7**
> **Surrender**
> True surrender is a victory, not a defeat. When you can embrace the unknown and find strength in your vulnerability, then you will know real freedom.

Comments:

Thoughts for the Week:

> A slave should not seek to be punished. However, when mistakes are made, a slave should seek to earn the privilege of being punished and forgiven. This privilege is earned by consenting to the punishment deemed appropriate by the Owner, demonstrating genuine remorse for the shortcoming, and making a sincere effort not to repeat the mistake in the future.

Comments:

> As you explore new areas of physical submission, don't overlook the emotional and spiritual aspects. These areas can provide you with as much fulfillment and satisfaction as you gain from physical acts of submission. As you grow and learn, you will find these areas will become more integrated and very often indistinguishable from each other.

Comments:

Writing Assignment #7
Characteristics Essential for Ownership

What qualities or character traits does an Owner need to have in order to gain your consent to serve? Name at least three of these qualities and explain why you feel they are important.

> **Guidepost #8**
> **Contentment**
> When you are content to be simply yourself and don't compare or compete, everyone will respect you.   -Lao Tzu

Comments:

Thoughts for the Week:

> Make an effort to understand each order and rule you are given. Why is the rule necessary? What does your Owner hope to achieve by assigning the task? What is the ultimate purpose of the rule? Knowing the answers to questions such as these will help you to comply with the spirit of the instructions as well as the specifics. Giving your Owner that extra level of obedience will add to the pleasure you both receive.

Comments:

> There is a time and place for everything. If you want to amuse your Owner by a display of "spunk" or "bratty" behavior, do so privately. There is a vast difference between public disrespect and private amusement.

Comments:

Writing Assignment #8
Personal Fantasy

Describe a personal fantasy you have not yet fulfilled.

> **Guidepost #9**
> **Pride**
> Pride is like food – too much or too little is unhealthy but the right amount gives us the energy we need to keep going.

Comments:

Thoughts for the Week:

> Make an effort to reach out to other slaves, even if it is from the safe anonymity of your computer. You will find that sharing experiences will help you learn from the mistakes of others. Also, the reassurance that others share similar thoughts and perspectives will help you to feel more at ease with your own choice to serve.

Comments:

> The time and attention your Owner chooses to give you is a privilege, not a right. This privilege needs to be earned, and once received, cherished.

Comments:

Writing Assignment #9
Self-Improvement

What is your greatest weakness as a slave? What are you doing to help improve that?

Monthly Practical Project #3
Travel Planning

Pretend that your Owner has decided that you both will take a two-week vacation and wishes to take a trip which includes visiting at least three cities. Your assignment is to plan the entire trip. Your plan should include: which cities you and your Owner will visit, transportation, lodging, meals, itinerary for each day of the vacation, and total cost. The goal for the vacation budget should be to have an enjoyable vacation that is still economical (pretend that every dollar saved goes into the "slave souvenir fund"). When planning the vacation, keep in mind what types of things your Owner doesn't mind cutting corners on and which luxuries your Owner would want to enjoy.

Research tool suggestions:
- AAA Tour Books
- Travel websites such as Orbitz and Travelocity
- Discount travel websites such as Hotels.com, Priceline, and Hotwire
- Tourist bureau websites

Ideas and Resources:

> **Guidepost #10**
> **Honor**
> No person was ever honored for what he received. Honor was the reward for what he gave. -Calvin Coolidge

Comments:

Thoughts for the Week:

> Be honest with yourself and your Owner about your needs as a slave. It is vital that you both have an understanding of what you require in order to gain pleasure and fulfillment from your submission. If these needs are neglected or not communicated, the quality of service you will be able to offer will be diminished.

Comments:

> Even the most tiresome and tedious of tasks can become pleasurable to perform over time. Initially, focus on the pleasure your Owner will gain from the finished product. Next, focus on the pleasure you give through your willing compliance and continued dedication to service. Finally, take pleasure from what you have learned, you accomplishments, and your added value as a slave.

Comments:

Writing Assignment #10
Reality Check

The reality of being a slave is very different than the fantasy. What are some of the things about being a slave that are different from what you imagined they would be.

> **Guidepost #11**
> **Integrity**
> Your actions are a reflection of your beliefs. Integrity comes when what you do matches what you believe.

Comments:

Thoughts for the Week:

> Remember when you were a child and tried to get something by claiming that "all the other parents let their kids"? Well, it probably didn't work then and you shouldn't try it now with your Owner. Service relationships are based on the personal preferences of the parties involved and do not follow a pre-ordained, universal standard. You have unique needs, wants and desires. Therefore, you should respect the unique standards and guidelines that your Owner imposes upon you.

Comments:

> In "vanilla" society, people are often judged by the company they keep – and this is even more prevalent in the Master/slave community. Your actions are a direct reflection on your Owner, the quality of training you have received, and the standards of behavior that have been set for you. It is up to you whether you are an asset or a liability to your owner.

Comments:

Writing Assignment #11
A Song in Your Heart

Name one song that you would sing to your Owner that would describe your relationship and explain why you have chosen that song. (If you are not in a relationship, what song describes how you would like to feel about your Owner.)

> **Guidepost #12**
> **Duty**
> Duty is the most sublime word in our language. Do your duty in all things.
> You cannot do more. You should never wish to do less.
> -Robert E. Lee

Comments:

Thoughts for the Week:

> There is no such thing as "just" as slave.

Comments:

> While it is not true that slaves should be seen and not heard, a quiet demeanor can be very beneficial to you. Remember, you cannot put your foot in your mouth if it remains closed.

Comments:

Writing Assignment #12
The Infamous Car Analogy Question

If people were cars, what kind of car would you be and why?

> **Guidepost #13**
> **Commitment**
> A person's life is limited but serving the people is limitless. I want to devote my limited life to serving the people limitlessly.
> -Ralph Waldo Emerson

Comments:

Thoughts for the Week:

> Pointing out the mistakes and shortcomings of others will not make you appear to be a better slave or worthy of respect by contrast. However, a tolerant and understanding slave will be praised and valued.

Comments:

> Showing respect to your Owners includes respecting his or her personal space. One example of this is a commonly practiced protocol that requires a slave to ask permission to touch his or her Owner. Whatever your protocols, you will take greater pleasure in being the presence of your Owner when you consider that it is a privilege that you have been granted because you have earned it.

Comments:

Writing Assignment #13
More Fantasy Exploration

Describe one of your fantasies that you have fulfilled.

Monthly Practical Project #4
Compiling a Packing List

Compile the packing list for the vacation you planned last month. Keep in mind the activities planned and expected weather conditions to decide what clothing will be needed. In addition to clothing, your packing list should include toiletries, medications, and any other items your Owner may wish to take on the vacation (such as camera, books or toys). If there are items on your list that your Owner does not currently possess, research the cost of those items so you can incorporate that into the vacation budget. (If you are not currently in service, pretend that your Owner needs to buy three articles of clothing, a pair of walking shoes, and two additional items.)

Suggested Research Tools:
- Weather.com
- Tourist bureau websites
- Travelers' tips websites

Ideas and Resources:

> **Guidepost #14**
> **Honesty**
> Self-reflection is the path to honesty. You must know yourself in order to be honest with yourself and you must be honest with yourself before you can be honest with others.

Comments:

Thoughts for the Week:

> Most of us spent years fantasizing about this lifestyle before we experienced the reality. We had an image in our mind of the "perfect Owner". We also had an image in our mind of how we would behave as the "perfect slave" if we had the "perfect owner". In reality, no one is perfect. You and your owner will make mistakes. You need to be willing to forgive yourself and your owner when that happens.

Comments:

> By going to the edge and back with your Owner, the bonds of trust between you are reaffirmed and strengthened.

Comments:

Writing Assignment #14
The Joy of Service

What do you enjoy most about performing service?

> **Guidepost #15**
> **Curiosity**
> A genuine desire to learn and grow is a quality that should be carefully nurtured. Feed your curiosity, but trim it back when it starts to overwhelm you.

Comments:

Thoughts for the Week:

> Every task you perform for your Owner frees up his or her time to do something else. It is important for you to understand what your Owner is doing with that time since you are, in effect, assisting in those efforts. This is just one reason why it is important for an Owner and a slave to have similar ethical values.

Comments:

> It is impossible to be completely honest with someone else unless you are honest with yourself first.

Comments:

Writing Assignment #15
In-depth Exploration—Integrity

Go to the dictionary and find the definition of "integrity". Pretend you are trying to explain "integrity" to someone who has never heard the word and write your own definition.

> **Guidepost #16**
> **Usefulness**
> How can I be useful, of what service can I be? There is something inside me, what can it be?   -Vincent Van Gogh

Comments:

Thoughts for the Week:

> Do not confuse an unwillingness to "take" control with a lack of strength or ability to handle Ownership. A good Owner will judiciously exercise control that is freely given; an abuser is one who will "take" it.

Comments:

> Many slaves make the mistake of thinking that they need to "act up" in order to gain the attention of their Owner. Even if this does gain you the attention you seek, it will not last long. The squeaky wheel may get the grease, but it will also be replaced at the first opportunity by one that works properly.

Comments:

Writing Assignment #16
First Impressions

What do you hope is the first thing people notice when they meet you?

Guidepost #17
Success
Savor your small victories and they will lead you to big ones.

Comments:

Thoughts for the Week:

> Accept the decisions made by your Owner with grace. If you have additional information that may change the outcome of the decision, then you should respectfully supply that information. Giving up control means agreeing to abide by decisions that you do not agree with – as well as the ones that you do. So, after you have informed your Owner of all the pertinent facts relating to the situation, be prepared to support whatever decision is made. Otherwise, the gift of trust you gave when agreeing to surrender is hollow and meaningless.

Comments:

> Just about anyone can be taught how to cook, clean a house, and provide physical service. It is a very special person, however, who can provide service for the heart and the soul.

Comments:

Writing Assignment #17
Receiving Compliments

What was the most recent compliment you received and how did it make you feel?

Guidepost #18
Growth
Change is inevitable. We either grow or we wither. I choose to grow.

Comments:

Thoughts for the Week:

> There is a saying that it is easier to get forgiveness than permission. While this may be true, it is not desirable conduct for a slave. If you know your Owner will not approve of your actions, you need to honor your commitment to abide by your Owner's rules. If you think there is a possibility that your Owner will not approve of something you would like to do, ask first.

Comments:

> Your Owner has offered you guidance, protection and comfort. If you hide your feelings or do not seek guidance, you are denying your Owner the pleasure that he or she gains from providing for your well-being. It is the same as if you were denied the pleasure you receive from serving.

Comments:

Writing Assignment #18
Memory Lane

Describe a time from your childhood when you performed a service.

Monthly Practical Project #5
Horticulture

Your Owner has decided to plant a garden. This month's assignment is for you to plan that garden. You will need to decide what type of garden to plant (vegetable, flower, herb, water, etc.) and how large the area of the garden will be. Make a list of what will be planted and decide how many of each type will be needed for the garden. You should account for your location climate when deciding on the plants for the garden. You will also need to research how to care for the plants you have selected for the garden. Finally, compile a list of tools needed to properly care for the garden.

Suggested Research Tools:
- Nursery websites
- HGTV.com and other home improvement websites
- Local nursery
- Local home improvement store

Ideas and Resources:

Guidepost #19
Courage
Face your fears, know the risks, and just go for it!

Comments:

Thoughts for the Week:

> One person's idea of a precious gift may be another person's idea of an unwanted burden. If the gift is not desirable, it will not be cherished.

Comments:

> I have often heard slaves try to justify their rudeness to others by stating, "I am only submissive to one person." Being polite and courteous to someone does not require submission; it merely requires that you be a kind, decent human being. There is also the mistaken belief that it somehow elevates your Owner in the eyes of others if he or she is the only one to whom you show respect. Your Owner is seen by others to be responsible for your actions; therefore, any offense you give to someone is also given by your Owner. It is not much of an accomplishment for your owner to own someone that no one else can tolerate.

Comments:

Writing Assignment #19
Real Role Models

Who is your real life role model as a slave and why?

> **Guidepost #20**
> **Stillness**
> The voice of the heart is soft. Take some time to find the stillness so your heart can be heard.

Comments:

Thoughts for the Week:

> Even if you consider yourself to be a natural slave, you will find it difficult at times to maintain the level of obedience and service you have consented to give. This is especially true as you first start your journey of self-exploration through a service relationship. Slavery requires more than just a natural desire – it requires the mental and physical discipline of training. Think of yourself as an artist who must learn the techniques necessary to make your vision a reality.

Comments:

> I find comfort and reassurance in the knowledge that I will be punished for my mistakes. The punishment I receive and the forgiveness that follows allow me the freedom to be human. It is a demonstration to me that I do not need to be perfect to be loved and valued.

Comments:

Writing Assignment #20
In-depth Exploration—Vulnerability

What does "being vulnerable" mean to you? Do you feel good or do you feel bad when you allow yourself to be vulnerable?

> **Guidepost #21**
> **Kindness**
> Kindness in words creates confidence. Kindness in thinking creates profundity. Kindness in giving creates love.   -Lao-Tzu

Comments:

Thoughts for the Week:

> Wouldn't it be nice if your car could tell you when it needs routine maintenance? What if your car could tell you what needs to be fixed when it is not running properly? You would probably get a lifetime of use and pleasure from a properly maintained car. Your Owner has agreed to take care of you and be responsible for your needs. This responsibility will become impossible to fulfill if you cannot or will not communicate what those needs are. The more adept you are at identifying and communicating those needs, the less of a burden you place on your owner.

Comments:

> Serving with quiet grace and dignity will do more to demonstrate the trust and respect you have for your owner than grand pronouncements of eternal slavery.

Comments:

Writing Assignment #21
In-Depth Exploration—Honor

Go to the dictionary and find the definition of "honor". Pretend you are trying to explain "honor" to someone who has never heard the word and write your own definition.

> **Guidepost #22**
> **Comfort**
> Give what you have. To someone, it may be better than you dare to think.
> –Henry Wadsworth Longfellow

Comments:

Thoughts for the Week:

> Being a good slave requires an extraordinary amount of patience. However, if you focus on trusting your Owner and having faith in yourself, you will find the keys to maintaining that level of patience necessary to fulfilling your commitment to slavery.

Comments:

> Ignorance is unattractive in anyone – including slaves. Constantly strive to learn and increase your awareness.

Comments:

Writing Assignment #22
Happiness

Describe a time in the past week when you were happy.

Monthly Practical Project #6
Budgeting and Economizing

Using the garden plan you developed in the previous project, put together a budget for the entire project. The budget should include cost of the plants, tools, and garden decorations (if any). After you have compiled your first budget, imagine that your Owner has told order you to reduce the budget amount by 25%. You can find less expensive alternatives to the plants you have chosen or find alternative sources to obtain the materials for the garden, but you should preserve as much of the original plan as possible.

Suggested Research Tools:
- E-bay
- Other auction websites
- Garden supply websites
- Price comparison websites

Ideas and Resources:

Guidepost #23
Joy
Never underestimate the value of laughter. Where there is laughter, there is joy. Where there is joy, there is no room for anger.

Comments:

Thoughts for the Week:

> Make sure you do not place burdens on your Owner that he or she has not consented to accept. For instance, if you retain control of your finances, then be prepared to accept the responsibility for your financial success or failure.

Comments:

> When I am allowed to see the passionate emotions of my Owner, I am thrilled by the intimacy and humbled by the trust that the intimacy demonstrates.

Comments:

Writing Assignment #23
A Song in My Heart—Part Two

What song would you most like to have your Owner (or future Owner) to sing to you and what makes that song special to you?

Guidepost #24
Acceptance
Embrace whatever you receive rather than mourning that which does not exist.

Comments:

Thoughts for the Week:

> Most of us did not grow up in a consensual service relationship household so we did not have role models for how to live in a healthy service relationship. Since we do not have observational experience to guide us, it is important to seek out information on real-life service relationships. This also means a service relationship will require more work in the beginning than a traditional relationship, so do not get discouraged when the relationship gets rocky.

Comments:

> If you do not show respect for the commitments made by others, then you diminish the significance of the commitment you have made to your owner.

Comments:

Writing Assignment #24
Self-Image

I feel sexiest when…. (fill in the blank and try to be descriptive)

> **Guidepost #25**
> **Willingness**
> Successful service requires willingness. It must be willingly given and willingly received.

Comments:

Thoughts for the Week:

> Slavery is not the pursuit of pain; it is the pursuit of pleasure through surrender and service. Sometimes that pleasure comes not from the act itself but from the joy of giving and the triumph of accomplishment.

Comments:

> When I am experiencing difficulties, usually the best way to resolve them is to shift my attention back to the simplest, basic tasks. Doing something – anything – improves my self-confidence because I feel useful and productive. With renewed confidence, the more complex problems are easier to overcome.

Comments:

Writing Assignment #25
First Impressions—Part Two

Think about someone you met or a stranger you observed in the past month who had a positive impact on you and describe the encounter.

> **Guidepost #26**
> Motivation
> Don't say that you want to give, but go ahead and give! You'll never catch up with a mere hope. -Johann Wolfgang von Goethe

Comments:

Thoughts for the Week:

> While trust and respect for your Owner are vital elements of your commitment to surrender, you should be willing to accept human failings from your Owner. Do not place him or her so high on a narrow pedestal that one misstep destroys your faith and trust.

Comments:

> Slaves often have a hard time saying "no" to others – not just to their Owner. Be aware of the primary commitments you have made so that you do not overextend yourself and end up failing those most important to you.

Comments:

Writing Assignment #26
Gratitude List

List five people or things you are grateful to have in your life and explain some of the reasons you value them so much.

Monthly Practical Project #7
Party Planning

Your Owner has decided to host a party for 40 people in the leather community. Your assignment for this project is to decide on a theme for the party, plan the menu, plan at least two activities for the party, and compile the budget for the party. When planning the budget, decide how much of each item on your menu you will need to feed 40 people and include the cost of paper products. If your planned activities include SM play, make sure you include safety equipment in the budget (such as basic first aid kit, cleaning products, tarps, etc.). When planning your activities, try to find activities that will encourage your guests to mingle and will appeal to both couples and singles. The activities can be anything from SM play to human buffet to formal dinner service.

Suggested Research Tools:
- Sam's Club, CostCo or similar warehouse store
- Party planning websites
- Home entertainment idea websites

Ideas and Resources:

> **Guidepost #27**
> **Fulfillment**
> It is one of the most beautiful compensations of life, that no man can sincerely try to help another without helping himself.
> –Ralph Waldo Emerson

Comments:

Thoughts for the Week:

> Don't be ashamed of your tears. They are products of your love.

Comments:

> Slavery is a powerful and beautiful gift to those who understand its value, but dangerous for those who do not. Surrendering to those who do not understand what they are receiving is like giving a child an expensive race car.

Comments:

Writing Assignment #27
Accomplishments

Describe something you feel proud to have accomplished.

> **Guidepost #28**
> **Inspiration**
> Who knows what happens when the pebble falls beneath the surface of the water? Small kindnesses may inspire great deeds.

Comments:

Thoughts for the Week:

> Slavery requires active participation. Even if you only consent to submit for a specified scene, you are more than just a target for someone's flogger. The more you give, the more you will get back.

Comments:

> Compliments should be given the same weight and consideration that you give to criticism and accepted graciously. Your gratitude and respect for the opinion of the person offering the praise will be better demonstrated through a commitment to justify the praise than by false modesty.

Comments:

Writing Assignment #28
In-depth Exploration—Usefulness

What makes you feel useful? Why?

> **Guidepost #29**
> **Responsibility**
> I will strive to acknowledge the consequences of my actions. I will accept praise when it is merited and I will make amends when I falter.

Comments:

Thoughts for the Week:

> I have an obligation to my Owner to take care of myself in his absence. I am his property and need to treat myself with the same respect and care I give to all his possessions

Comments:

> You have blindfolded me so that I can see more clearly, you have silenced me so that I can speak more eloquently, and you have bound me so that I can have true freedom.

Comments:

Writing Assignment #29
Once Upon a Time...

What is your favorite erotic story or book? Why?

> **Guidepost #30**
> **Experience**
> Knowledge can be gained in many ways but the path to wisdom resides in experience.

Comments:

Thoughts for the Week:

> As you learn and grow as a person, your needs and wants as a slave will change. It is important to communicate these changes and renegotiate the framework of your relationship to reflect your new needs. The renegotiation process can be stressful, but the stress will be minimized if you view it as a result of success in personal awareness rather than a failure by either party to anticipate the changes you are destined to undergo.

Comments:

> Slavery requires patience. It is not the path for those who seek instant gratification. It is the road for those who take pleasure in the journey and find contentment in the knowledge that the road never ends.

Comments:

Writing Assignment #30
Teachers

Who was your favorite teacher when you were in school? What made that person special to you?

> **Guidepost #31**
> Excellence
> The greatest virtues are those which are most useful to other persons.
> -Aristotle

Comments:

Thoughts for the Week:

> One cannot truly serve, no matter how skillfully tutored, without doing so out of love and compassion.

Comments:

> Take responsibility for your mistakes — even if you are the only one who would ever know about them. A lie by omission is still a lie and demonstrates a lack of faith in your Owner's ability to forgive.

Comments:

Writing Assignment #31
Self-Knowledge

Describe something you have learned about yourself within the past two months.

Monthly Practical Project #8
Dungeon Decor

Your Owner has decided to turn one bedroom into a dungeon/playroom. Your assignment for this project is to design the playroom. You will need to decide on a style or theme for the room and identify two pieces of equipment for the playroom (one large and one small piece). In addition to the play equipment, you will need to plan the artwork, decorations, and other accessories for the playroom. When planning the décor, don't forget the paint, window treatments, lighting, and other hardware for the room. In addition to the play equipment and décor, you will need to compile a list of items needed to address health and safety issues. Finally, you will need to compile the budget for the entire project.

Suggested Research Tools:
- Dungeon equipment websites
- Fetish and erotic art websites
- Dungeon Monitor Guides
- BDSM Safety websites

Ideas and Resources:

> **Guidepost #32**
> **Grace**
> Grace is the ability to make the most complicated tasks appear effortless to the untrained eye.

Comments:

Thoughts for the Week:

> No one wants to fail. However, failures can be turned into successes if you take the time to analyze why the failure occurred and take steps to insure that it does not happen in the future. Mistakes are inevitable, but foresight and hindsight should be used to reduce their frequency.

Comments:

> An Owner can be many things to a slave – a lover, a friend, an authority figure, and a protector just to name a few. However, an Owner is not a substitute for a therapist if that is what you need.

Comments:

Writing Assignment #32
Dream Job

Describe your dream job and explain why you would want to do it.

> **Guidepost #33**
> **Loyalty**
> Great services are not canceled by one act or by one single error.
> –Benjamin Disraeli

Comments:

Thoughts for the Week:

> There will be times when you get discouraged or feel resentful of the expectations of your Owner. This is not necessarily an indication of a lack of dedication on your part; more likely it is an indication that you are doing too much too soon or your needs are not being met. Whatever the cause, it is important that you communicate your difficulties to your Owner so the two of you can work out a solution to the problem.

Comments:

> Only when I allow myself to be vulnerable can I experience the fulfillment that comes from having my trust in another verified.

Comments:

Writing Assignment #33
Book Report

What was the last book you read? What made you want to read it? Did you enjoy it?

> **Guidepost #34**
> **Confidence**
> Success is contagious. Help others achieve their goals and you will find the confidence to achieve your own.

Comments:

Thoughts for the Week:

> Training a slave requires an enormous commitment of time and energy from an Owner. In order for training to be successful, the Owner and the slave must work together. By applying yourself diligently to the training regimen set for you, the burden on your Owner is reduced.

Comments:

> Do not judge yourself as a slave by the standards set by others. When you are uncertain about a course of action, seek counsel from your Owner. If you have pleased your Owner, then you need not concern yourself with the opinions of others.

Comments:

Writing Assignment #34
Physical Delights

What food would you most like to eat off of someone else's body? What part of the body would you use as your "plate"? Why?

> **Guidepost #35**
> **Elegance**
> Moving through life, silently and seamlessly, providing pleasure to those who did not know it was missing until they experienced it.

Comments:

Thoughts for the Week:

> It is vital in a service relationship for both parties to give informed consent. If you are not honest with your Owner about your feelings, expectations, and actions then you are getting his or her consent under false pretenses. You are, in effect, practicing nonconsensual activities when you lie or withhold information.

Comments:

> Slavery requires a great amount of self-discipline. The structure, guidelines, and rules set by your Owner provide a framework of support, rather than a substitute, for your own self-discipline.

Comments:

Writing Assignment #35
Fantasy Owner

What fictional character would you most like to own you? Why?

Monthly Practical Project #9
Preparing to Attend a Leather Event

Your Owner has decided that you both will attend a weekend-long leather event in a different city. Your assignment for this project is to choose an event, plan the travel arrangements, compile a packing list, and compile a budget for the weekend. When compiling the packing list, take into account the types of activities planned for the weekend (dungeon party, formal banquet, bar crawl, etc.) as well as the expected weather conditions during the event. When determining the budget for the weekend, don't forget to include meals, tips, airport parking, shuttles/taxis, etc. After you have compiled the budget for the weekend, imagine that your Owner has decided that every dollar you can trim out of the proposed budget will be spent in the vendor area and try to find less expensive (but not too inconvenient) options for meals and travel.

Suggested Research Tools:
- Travel websites such as Orbitz and Travelocity
- Discount travel websites such as Hotels.com and Hotwire
- Leather event calendar websites
- Leather event websites

Ideas and Resources:

> **Guidepost #36**
> **Creativity**
> If you can imagine a pathway, you can find a way to follow it. Sometimes the best reason to do something is simply that no one has ever tried it.

Comments:

Thoughts for the Week:

> One of the most valuable services you can do for your Owner is to be an interested listener. An interested listener is someone who pays attention to what is being said and asks questions in order to understand what the other person is saying. Try not to distract your Owner from the main point, but ask for clarification or background information when you start to get confused.

Comments:

> Self-confidence gives me the ability to relinquish control.

Comments:

Writing Assignment #36
A Different Perspective

If your bed could talk, what would it say about you?

> **Guidepost #37**
> **Dignity**
> There is a healthful hardiness about real dignity that never dreads contact and communion with others, however, humble.
> –Washington Irving

Comments:

Thoughts for the Week:

> There will be some skills that you will never fully acquire. Instead of perfection, aim for competence in those cases. We can't all be concert pianists but we can all learn to make music in some form.

Comments:

> There is a common misconception that slavery requires giving up personal power. Unfortunately, a powerless slave is not very useful. However, a slave who has a sense of his or her own personal power is like a turbo-charged power tool – turbo-charged, but still under the control of their Owner.

Comments:

Writing Assignment #37
In-depth Exploration—Respect

Go to the dictionary and find the definition of "respect". Pretend you are trying to explain "respect" to someone who has never heard the word and write your own definition.

Guidepost #38
Dreams
Go confidently in the direction of your dreams. Live the life you have imagined.   –Henry David Thoreau

Comments:

Thoughts for the Week:

> There is true freedom in total surrender. Expectations and fears are our only real shackles.

Comments:

> A collar is a symbol of the commitment between you and your Owner. It is a tangible reminder to both of you that the relationship is consensual. As long as you feel that collar around your neck, you know that your Owner is still willing to abide by the terms set for your relationship. Wearing your collar demonstrates to your Owner that you are still willing to surrender control.

Comments:

Writing Assignment #38
Physical Examination

List what you think are your five best physical attributes and explain why.

> **Guidepost #39**
> **Faith**
> Faith is a rare loving strength that is a blessing to have even when it hurts to keep it.

Comments:

Thoughts for the Week:

> Grace in movement comes when you are at ease within your body and your physical surroundings. Grace in action comes when you are at ease within your heart.

Comments:

> Honor and integrity are the ethical qualities that compel us to behave as if our Owners were right beside us even if they are half a world away.

Comments:

Writing Assignment #39
Say What?

Be creative. Think of your own writing assignment and complete it.

Monthly Practical Project #10
Fetish Attire

Your Owner has decided that you both need new clothing for the leather event you chose in the previous project. Your assignment for this project is to decide what items you will purchase for your Owner and for yourself. You can spend 20% of your final event budget amount on your Owner and 10% of the final budget amount on yourself.

Suggested Research Tools:
- E-bay
- Fetish Auctioneer
- Fetish clothing websites

Ideas and Resources:

> **Guidepost #40**
> **Gratitude**
> Serving others reminds me of my gratitude for the gifts I have to offer others.

Comments:

Thoughts for the Week:

> There is a very good reason why service relationships are referred to as "power exchange relationships" rather than "power drain relationships". If you do not feel empowered by your relationship, you need to examine the reasons why you feel this way and work with your Owner to correct the situation.

Comments:

> I have found that the biggest obstacle I face is my own insecurity. When I am feeling insecure, my actions are tentative and my feelings are easily hurt. When I am feeling confident, my actions are purposeful and I do not let little things diminish my happiness.

Comments:

Writing Assignment #40
Seven Little Words

List seven words that describe you and explain why you think they are applicable.

Guidepost #41
Listen
Hearing is an act of the body. Listening is an act of the heart.

Comments:

Thoughts for the Week:

> My goal as a slave is to have the glass of water in my Owner's hand before he even knows he is thirsty ... and without him even noticing that I put it there.

Comments:

> Owners and slaves often joke about Owners being able to "see all and know all". We all consciously admit that this is not the case, but sometimes slaves will hold a subconscious belief that this is true. While this is a wonderful testament to the respect the slave has for the Owner, it can be dangerous for the relationship. The communication necessary to maintain the relationship will suffer because the slave will expect that the Owner already knows whatever it is that needs to be communicated. Worse, the slave will sometimes resent the Owner for not knowing something that the slave failed to communicate. So, if there is something your Owner needs to know, speak up. Owners can "know all and see all", but only if their slaves keep them informed.

Comments:

Writing Assignment #41
Civil Disobedience?

Is it ever acceptable for a slave to disobey orders? Why or why not?

> **Guidepost #42**
> **Empowerment**
> Give light, and the darkness will disappear of itself.
> –Desiderus Erasmus

Comments:

Thoughts for the Week:

> Impatience stems from a fear of the unknown. Trust and faith in your Owner are the most potent weapons against impatience.

Comments:

> I do not serve my Owner because he is unwilling or unable to take care of himself. I serve my Owner in order to free his time to accomplish his goals. I share his vision of what the world should be. By serving him, I am serving our goals.

Comments:

Writing Assignment #42
Submission and Surrender

In your opinion, what is the difference between submission and surrender?

Guidepost #43
Passion
Illuminate your path by releasing your passion and letting it lead you.

Comments:

Thoughts for the Week:

> I know a slave who was told, "You will never make a good slave because you are too intelligent, too stubborn and too sarcastic." I do not believe those are negative qualities for a slave to possess. An intelligent slave is a valuable asset to any Owner, a stubborn slave will keep going in the face of adversity, and a sarcastic slave can be a source of amusement for an Owner under the right circumstances.

Comments:

> Stillness of the mind is the first stage of opening the soul. When the mind is still, the soul hears the voice of the heart.

Comments:

Writing Assignment #43
Love

I need to be loved by my Owner. Do you agree or disagree with this statement? Why?

Monthly Practical Project #11
Single-tail Whips

Your Owner has decided to buy a single-tail whip. Your assignment for this project is to research single-tail whips in order to assist in the purchase and care for the whip after the purchase. Your research should include types of single-tail whips, how they are constructed, what to look for when buying a whip, where to buy a single-tail whip (you should identify at least four suppliers), single-tail whip safety, and how to care for the whip.

Suggested Research Tools:
- Whip maker websites
- Whip users websites

Ideas and Resources:

> **Guidepost #44**
> **Progress**
> Savor each step you take toward your goal. The joy is in the journey, not the destination.

Comments:

Thoughts for the Week:

> Since the goal of seamless service is for the slave to be unnoticeable there may be times when a very good slave will feel unappreciated. When that happens, take heart that it is a positive reflection on your abilities as a slave. In the absence of positive attention, the temptation to provoke a negative reaction from your Owner in order to get the attention you seek can be very hard to resist. Therefore, it is important to let your Owner know if you feel you need more attention. Sometimes a short conversation can avert a big disaster.

Comments:

> I am not forced to serve because I am incapable of pursuing my own goals.
> I choose to serve because I am capable of pursuing my own goals.

Comments:

Writing Assignment #44
You've Got Personality!

List three things about your personality that you feel help make you a good slave and explain why?

> **Guidepost #45**
> **Perfection**
> If you can see perfection within others, then know that they can see it within you.

Comments:

Thoughts for the Week:

> There will be times when you are not able to directly serve your Owner, but you can always find ways to serve indirectly. For instance, if you are escorting your Owner to a business function, you can wear something specifically because you know your Owner enjoys seeing you in it, you can mingle and network for your Owner, or you can even get that last piece of shrimp on the buffet and discreetly offer it to your Owner. Use your imagination and the possibilities are endless.

Comments:

> There are people in this world whose souls are moved by experiencing devoted service. Cherish those people whether they are known as Masters, as slaves, or any other label.

Comments:

Writing Assignment #45
The Gift of Giving

Describe a special gift someone gave you. What made it special for you?

> **Guidepost #46**
> **Change**
> I can't go back to yesterday ... because I was a different person then.
> -Lewis Carroll

Comments:

Thoughts for the Week:

> I have found that my ability to trust someone else is directly related to my self-confidence. When I am feeling strong and powerful, I eagerly embrace opportunities to be vulnerable and trusting. When I doubt myself, I start doubting those around me.

Comments:

> Try to keep a proper perspective on everything your Owner asks you to do. Some tasks are fun, some are chores, and some are vitally important. Life can be stressful enough without adding unnecessary burdens.

Comments:

Writing Assignment #46
Taking a Stand

Describe an incident where you stood up for your beliefs. What happened?

Guidepost #47
Trust
Service begins when trust is given and ends when trust is broken.

Comments:

Thoughts for the Week:

> If I do not expect to go to a movie, I am not disappointed if my Owner chooses to spend the evening at home. On the other hand, our trust in our Owners requires that we hold on to some expectations. If my Owner says that we are going to a movie, then my commitment to trust requires that I accept that expectation and the risk of disappointment.

Comments:

> Service is a gift that you offer. To have that gift accepted is an honor and a privilege.

Comments:

Writing Assignment #47
Peace

I feel at peace when…(be as descriptive as possible)

> **Guidepost #48**
> **Needs**
> Honor your needs. They provide the fuel to live your life and you're your passions.

Comments:

Thoughts for the Week:

> Try not to fall into the trap of having an "I'm not that kind of slave" attitude. This attitude is usually a sign that you are uncertain about your ability to succeed in a particular area. If you demonstrate a willingness to try, your efforts will be appreciated whether you are successful or not.

Comments:

> Whenever possible, choose joy.

Comments:

Writing Assignment #48
Santa's Workshop

If you were one of Santa's elves, what job would you like to have and why?

Monthly Practical Project #12
Basic Massage Skills

All of the time spent practicing with the new single-tail has made your Owner's muscles sore. Your assignment for this project is to learn how to give a massage. You should choose a particular style and research the philosophy, technique and medical considerations for that style. If you are already familiar with massage techniques, find a style that you have not studied and research that style. You should also compile a list of the equipment needed for the massage (massage table, oils, etc.).

Suggested Research Tools:
- Massage websites
- Books on massage techniques
- Community college classes

Ideas and Resources:

> **Guidepost #49**
> **Sacrifice**
> For anything worth having, one must pay the price; and the price is always work, patience, love, self-sacrifice – no paper currency, no promises to pay, but the gold of real service. —John Burroughs

Comments:

Thoughts for the Week:

> How do you know if you have become truly Owned in your heart? It is different for each slave. I knew I was completely Owned when I realized that I would do everything in my power to satisfy my Owner's needs, wants and desires. Even when my conscious mind was saying "no", my subconscious mind was trying to figure out a way to say "yes".

Comments:

> Slavery is a journey, and the only way to buy a ticket for the trip is to trust.

Comments:

Writing Assignment #49
In-depth Exploration—Obedience

Do you like being told what to do? Why or why not?

> **Guidepost #50**
> **Forgiveness**
> Forgiveness is the scent that the violet sheds on the heel that has crushed it.
> –Mark Twain

Comments:

Thoughts for the Week:

> A good skill to have is the ability to keep your focus centered on your Owner while staying out of your Owner's line of sight. This is the key to anticipatory service. The problem with perfecting this skill is that being invisible can be a lonely experience. Just remember that the invisibility is an illusion. Your Owner may not visibly notice your presence, but your absence would definitely be noticed.

Comments:

> An old tool for self-improvement is to "act as if". Decide what you would like others to see when they look at you and "act as if" they do. As long as your vision does not violate the laws of physics, in time you will become what you have envisioned yourself to be.

Comments:

Writing Assignment #50
Print or Film?

Would you rather read a book or watch a movie? Why?

Guidepost #51
Purpose
Serving without purpose is like eating cookies for breakfast.

Comments:

Thoughts for the Week:

> One problem slaves face is the conflict between giving up control and maintaining personal responsibility for one's actions. Just because you are ordered to do something does not mean you are not responsible for the consequences of your actions. A slave who is given an order to do something that the slave feels is morally wrong faces an ethical dilemma. To disobey the order, the slave has to violate the commitment made to obey the Owner. To obey the order, the slave has to violate his/her personal values. If that situation arises, discuss your concerns with your Owner. There is no right or wrong answer to the dilemma; it is simply a matter of deciding which path you feel most comfortable taking.

Comments:

> When words fail you, let go and let your spirit speak for you.

Comments:

Writing Assignment #51
Rebellion

Describe a time when you disagreed with an authority figure (teacher, boss, parent, Owner, etc.). What did you do and how did you feel afterwards?

> **Guidepost #52**
> **Guideposts**
> What inspires you? What motivates you? What is inside you that you want to show the world? What is it that brings you peace when you are troubled? Look to these things to find your own special guideposts.

Comments:

Thoughts for the Week:

> Surrendering to your Owner is not an admission of defeat or personal inadequacy. True surrender requires the courage to face the unknown and trust in the guide you have chosen to lead you into the unexplored territory. When you have found within yourself the courage and trust required to surrender that is a victory to savor.

Comments:

A Slave's Creed
(alter as necessary to fit your own beliefs)

- I am independent.
- I am intelligent.
- I am capable of running my own life – and I am responsible for running those parts of my life that my Owner does not wish to run.
- I find my greatest personal satisfaction comes from service.
- I do not choose to serve simply because I "couldn't cut it as a Top".
- I feel empowered by service.
- I can withdraw my consent to my relationship with my Owner at any time but I choose to honor my commitments.
- I do not have a victim complex and I find being used or abused unacceptable – but I need to feel useful.
- I do not like being told what to do – I take pride in knowing what needs to be done without being told.
- My Owner does recognize my ownership of certain property, but there is nothing that I own that my heart would deny him if he desired it.
- I am my Owner's most prized possession.

Comments:

Writing Assignment #52
Looking Back

Look over the writing assignments you've completed. How many did you enjoy doing? What made an assignment easy or difficult for you?

Choosing To Serve

Several years ago, I was asked the question, "What response would you give to a feminist who feels that your lifestyle is counter-productive to women's movement?" My response was that I am very grateful to the women who fought to change the way our society views women since I have directly benefited from those changes in my personal and professional life. However, one of the main philosophies of the women's movement is that women should have the same freedom to choose how to live their lives as men. My choice to become a slave was simply my way of exercising that freedom.

On the surface, my life as a slave may not seem any different from the stereotypical 1950s housewife, but the similarities end when you look beneath the surface. Fifty years ago, women were expected to serve their husbands and families and they received little or no praise and recognition for their efforts. Women who pursued careers or other interests faced varying degrees of criticism and scorn for making those choices. My Masters knew that I fulfill my duties and responsibilities as a slave by choice; they recognized and appreciated my service as a gift. Also, my Masters appreciated my decision even more since they knew I chose to defy society in order to serve as their slave.

Each person who chooses to lead a service lifestyle has a different story about the path that led to that decision. My story is a bit more ironic than others. In 1996, I was in the process of getting a divorce and had just moved to a new city. For the first time in my life, I was living alone and did not have to answer to anyone for my decisions. I decided to take this opportunity to explore some of the sexual fantasies I had kept to myself for many years and I contacted the local BDSM group. At the time, I was not part of the "cyber age" and I knew nothing of the organized BDSM community. So when I attended my first meeting, I was a bit afraid that I would be walking into a starring role in a gangbang. Instead, I sat in a café and shared intimate details of my secret desires with three total strangers (and I'm still not sure I'm relieved or disappointed that my visions of a gangbang never materialized).

At that first meeting, I said that I was just looking to find someone to have fun with in the bedroom. I was not looking for a committed relationship and I certainly wouldn't consider doing this outside of the bedroom. I told them that I was too independent to be a full-time slave. Besides, for the first time in my life I had complete control over my own life, so why would I want to give that control to someone else? Three months later I met Master Scott at the group meeting. To make a long story short, I quickly discovered that I could not turn on and off my desire to serve him and I became his slave less than a month after our first meeting.

My feelings for Master Scott provided the catalyst for my decision to become a slave, but I realize in retrospect that I have always had what some call "slave heart". When I care about someone, I show affection and respect through service. It is not in my nature to say "no". A Master/slave relationship is actually one of the healthiest types of relationship for me since a Master understands that a slave will give until there is nothing left. A good Master knows how to channel that desire to serve so that a slave's full potential is reached but does not allow the slave to burn out in the process. My Masters knew that I would do my best to give them anything they asked from me and sometimes that knowledge kept them from asking at all. Given what I know

now about slaves and about myself, it is ironic but not surprising that when I was at a point in my life where I could choose to do anything, I chose to serve.

Two years after I met Master Scott, I met Master Todd. Just as I had experienced with Master Scott, I felt the desire to serve Master Todd from the first night I met him. By this time, however, I had enough experience to immediately recognize what I was feeling. Since I was already owned, the decision to serve Master Todd was not mine to make. I expressed my desire to Master Scott and after several months of negotiation, he allowed me to enter into a service relationship with Master Todd. For the first six years of our relationship, my service to Master Todd was intermittent. We only saw each other five or six times a year; some of those times I was in service to him and some of those times I was in what we called "buddy mode", where we treated each other as friends. There were some on-going aspects to my service relationship with Master Todd during that time, but even those were subject to change based on time and circumstances. In late 2004, however, Master Todd accepted an offer of co-ownership from Master Scott and we entered into a Master/slave relationship.

Neither Master Scott nor Master Todd required me to serve as a condition of having an intimate relationship with them. Master Scott and I started out just being "friends with benefits". I quickly realized, however, that the way I felt about him made me want to serve him and I was the one who requested the change in our relationship. When I met Master Todd, I was already in a fulfilling Master/slave relationship so I was not looking to find something to fill a void in my life. Again, it was how I felt about Master Todd that made me want to serve him so that was the relationship dynamic Master Scott negotiated for me. Also, in both cases, I did not require that they accept my offer of service in order to pursue a relationship. I would have been interested in any type of relationship with either of them, I was just fortunate that they both wanted an intimate service relationship with me.

I think it is important to note that I did not choose to be a slave because I couldn't take care of myself or make sound decisions for myself. If I couldn't take care of myself, I certainly couldn't be expected to take off and serve another person. If I couldn't make sound decisions, then I shouldn't be making as important a decision as whether or not to become a slave. I also did not become a slave because I felt I was inferior to the people I serve. If I had such a low opinion of myself, I would never have offered an inferior gift to two men I admire and respect. I chose to become a slave because I wanted to offer my talents and resources to serve these two men in whatever fashion they desired.

Even though each person will experience a different process that leads to the decision to serve, I think the reasons for making that decision should be basically the same for all. If you are considering a life of service, here are some questions to ask yourself:

Why do I want to serve?

You should have a clear understanding of why you want to live a service lifestyle. If you are making this decision with a particular person in mind, you should have concrete reasons for why you want to serve that person.

How will a service lifestyle benefit me?

A service lifestyle should never be confused with being a victim or a martyr. If you are not benefiting from the situation, you will quickly burn out and not be useful to anyone—including yourself. You should be able to identify the physical, emotional and spiritual benefits you expect to receive as a result of your service.

Do I respect people who are in service professions?

How you view others can provide a very clear picture of how you view yourself. If you feel pity for someone in a service profession who takes pride in their job, then you may want to examine how you feel about yourself.

Am I able to incorporate a service lifestyle into my current life situation?

You need to consider the impact on children, career, marriage, family, friends, and personal commitments. While none of these factors would eliminate the possibility of a service relationship, they will determine how that relationship needs to be structured. If you cannot accept the limitations imposed by your other commitments and be fulfilled by your service then you need to consider alternatives.

What are my personal life goals?

We all have things we would like to do or accomplish in our lives. Sometimes our goals are as simple as being a good friend to others or as complicated as finding a cure for cancer. Identifying your goals will help you determine whether a service lifestyle will help or hinder your efforts to achieve your goals. You may find that your goals would be most compatible with a particular type of person or service relationship.

Do I view a service lifestyle as a new challenge to undertake or as an escape from my personal difficulties?

As anyone who lives a service lifestyle can tell you, it is not easy. When you are in service to someone, you are not only responsible for serving them but you are still responsible for taking care of yourself. If you can't take care of yourself, you shouldn't be offering to take care of someone else.

(Note: I do recognize that there is a difference between doing something for yourself and doing something for others. I will procrastinate about doing my own dishes but I will happily offer to do the dishes when someone cooks a meal for me. However, it is not much of a service to cook someone a meal just to get them to clean up your kitchen.)

What do I have to offer in a service relationship?

Service goes far beyond sex and housework. Making a list of your skills and talents will give you a clear picture of whether what you have to offer will be useful to the person you wish to serve.

What will I need in order to be fulfilled by service?

It will be very helpful to the person you are serving if you can identify what you need in order to stay motivated to serve. Instead of making broad statements such as "I need appreciation" or "I need guidance", be as specific as possible since there are many ways to meet those needs but not all of them will work for you. Do you need to hear "thank you" or is a smile and a nod enough to melt your heart?

About The Author

Christina "slavette" Parker has balanced multiple relationships and several alternative lifestyles since 1996. Best known for her work in the leather and BDSM communities, she was a collared slave from 1996-2009. With her first Master, Christina was honored to receive the Pantheon of Leather Awards for Couple of the Year (2001) and Small Event of the Year for Together in Leather 2004 as well as hold the title of International slave 2002.

As part of her commitment to community service and activism, Christina has served as Fundraising Director for the National Coalition for Sexual Freedom (NCSF), served on the Board of Directors for CUFF, SSCN and Gnosis, and has been a founding member of four BDSM educational/support/social groups.

Christina has given over 200 workshops across the U.S. and in Canada. She was an instructor for Apex Academy/Butchman's Experience in Phoenix, AZ and serves as a guest instructor for Master Taino's Training Academy as needed. While she speaks on a variety of topics, her primary educational focus is on M/s relationships, service, polyamorous relationships, sacred sexuality, and spirituality. Christina is the author of *Many Hearts, Many Loves, Many Possibilities: The Polyamory Relationship Workbook* and is a columnist for Sexis Magazine.

www.ingramcontent.com/pod-product-compliance
Ingram Content Group UK Ltd.
Pitfield, Milton Keynes, MK11 3LW, UK
UKHW051302180426
11947UKWH00020B/1861